Do MUSIC AND ART Classes Matter?

By Robert M. Hamilton

Published in 2019 by
KidHaven Publishing, an Imprint of Greenhaven Publishing, LLC
353 3rd Avenue
Suite 255
New York, NY 10010

Designer: Deanna Paternostro
Editor: Katie Kawa

Photo credits: Cover, p. 19 SpeedKingz/Shutterstock.com; p. 5 (top) Pressmaster/Shutterstock.com; pp. 5 (bottom), 11, 21 (inset, middle-left) Monkey Business Images/Shutterstock.com; p. 7 Maria Dryfhout/Shutterstock.com; p. 9 Glen Martin/Contributor/Denver Post/Getty Images; p. 13 AVAVA/Shutterstock.com; p. 15 Rawpixel.com/Shutterstock.com; p. 17 Syda Productions/Shutterstock.com; p. 21 (notepad) ESB Professional/Shutterstock.com; p. 21 (markers) Kucher Serhii/Shutterstock.com; p. 21 (photo frame) FARBAI/iStock/Thinkstock; p. 21 (inset, left) Prostock-studio/Shutterstock.com; p. 21 (inset, middle-right) adriaticfoto/Shutterstock.com; p. 21 (inset, right) kreatorex/Shutterstock.com.

Cataloging-in-Publication Data

Names: Hamilton, Robert M.
Title: Do music and art classes matter? / Robert M. Hamilton.
Description: New York : KidHaven Publishing, 2019. | Series: Points of view | Includes glossary and index.
Identifiers: ISBN 9781534525689 (pbk.) | 9781534525672 (library bound) | ISBN 9781534525696 (6 pack) | ISBN 9781534525702 (ebook)
Subjects: LCSH: Arts–Juvenile literature. | Art–Technique–Juvenile literature. | Music–Instruction and study–Juvenile.
Classification: LCC NX633.H36 2019 | DDC 700–dc23

Printed in the United States of America

CPSIA compliance information: Batch #BS18KL: For further information contact Greenhaven Publishing LLC, New York, New York at 1-844-317-7404.

Please visit our website, www.greenhavenpublishing.com. For a free color catalog of all our high-quality books, call toll free 1-844-317-7404 or fax 1-844-317-7405.

CONTENTS

Cutting Creative
CLASSES

Do you take music and art classes? These classes, which are part of a group of classes often known as arts education, allow students to learn new things in a creative way.

Many people believe music and art classes play an important part in the lives of students. However, when schools need to save money, music and art **programs** are often cut. This is because some people believe art and music matter less than other classes. Different opinions about art and music can **affect** the future of arts education, so it's important to understand these points of view.

Know the Facts!

Dance and theater classes are often considered part of arts education too.

Art and music classes matter to many students, but some people argue they can be cut to save money and spend more time on other subjects. Before taking part in this **debate**, it's good to know all the facts so you can have an informed, or educated, opinion.

Arts Education by the
NUMBERS

Major studies on arts education in the United States don't happen very often. In 2012, the U.S. government presented the results of the first arts education study in 10 years. It showed how many students were missing out on a well-rounded education because they couldn't take any art or music classes.

According to the study, more than 1.3 million students in elementary schools weren't able to take music classes. Around 4 million elementary students weren't able to take art classes. There was also a large drop in the number of elementary schools offering theater and dance classes.

Know the Facts!

The U.S. Department of Education is the part of the U.S. government that collects facts and conducts studies about schools in the United States.

Schools cut art and music classes for different reasons. Understanding those reasons and trying to address them in new ways could help keep music and art classes in schools.

Money

MATTERS

Most people believe music and art classes matter and should be a part of a student's education. In some cases, though, budget cuts, which are cuts to the amount of money a school can use, cause people to question the importance of art and music classes over other classes.

Some people argue that art and music classes require too much money for things such as art supplies and instruments. They believe that money should be spent on things such as new science or math books, which are often seen as more useful for future jobs.

Know the Facts!

In 2017, members of the U.S. Senate voted to give $29 million more to the U.S. Department of Education than the department was given the year before.

Sometimes teachers and students raise money on their own to keep art and music programs in their schools. They often do this through events such as bake sales.

Discovering New
TALENTS

When people are faced with school budget cuts, they often make choices based on what they believe will help students get good jobs later in life. Some people believe music and art classes are less useful in this way than other classes. However, many companies want to hire creative people, and art and music classes help students become more creative.

Art and music classes also help students find reasons to enjoy school if they don't like classes such as math, science, or social studies. They help students find new talents and ways to be successful.

Know the Facts!

Students from **low-income** households who take art or music classes are five times less likely to drop out of, or quit, school than students who have no arts education.

Art and music classes are sometimes the reason students want to go to school. They teach students the value of different skills and talents, such as creativity.

Hard
CHOICES

Art and music classes are often in danger of being cut in schools in low-income neighborhoods. These schools often don't have a lot of money, so the people in charge have to make hard choices about how to use and save the money they're given.

In some cases, people make the choice to cut art and music classes so they can have money to pay more teachers for subjects such as reading and math. This keeps class sizes from being too big, which is often a problem in schools in big cities.

Know the Facts!

As of 2014, 20 percent of public schools in New York City had no arts education teachers, and 42 percent of schools without those teachers were in low-income areas of the city.

Some people believe schools should be **focused** on helping students in subjects such as math rather than on helping students in subjects such as music or art.

A Brighter FUTURE

Although schools in low-income areas often don't have money for arts education, studies have shown music and art can play a big part in helping students who live in these areas. When students from low-income neighborhoods are able to take art and music classes, they have better grades than those who aren't able to take them.

A national study of arts education in **low-performing** schools, which are often in low-income areas, was conducted in 2015. In this study, schools that began offering art and music classes had higher test scores and better attendance rates than they did before.

Know the Facts!

A national study of arts education showed that **at-risk** teenagers who took part in the arts in some way were more likely to go to **college** than those who weren't involved in the arts.

Offering art and music classes makes it more likely that students in low-income schools will continue with their education, which gives them more opportunities to succeed in the future.

The Trouble with TESTING

Some schools cut music and art classes to save time. They want to give students more time to prepare for standardized tests in subjects such as science, math, and reading. These are tests that are taken and graded in a consistent way to allow graders to compare students based on their test scores.

As standardized tests have become more important, subjects that aren't tested, such as art and music, are sometimes given less attention. Some people believe leaders who decide on education **policies** have made preparing for tests more important than thinking creatively.

Know the Facts!

As of 2016, at least six states were working to come up with standardized tests in the arts.

It takes a lot of time to prepare students for standardized tests. In some cases, teachers use the time that once belonged to music and art classes to get students ready for these tests.

Better
GRADES

Music and art classes can give students reasons to enjoy school if they don't like other subjects. Studies have shown that music and art classes can help students raise their grades in other subjects too.

Children who take music classes have higher math and English test scores than those who don't, and music classes have been shown to help with language **development** and memory. Also, students who take art classes have been shown to be four times more likely to be recognized for doing well in school than those who don't take art classes.

Know the Facts!

For many years, schools have focused on STEM subjects—science, technology, engineering, and math. However, today, some schools are changing that focus to STEAM, which brings the arts into STEM.

Music and art classes help students develop the skills they need to succeed in other subjects, such as math and English.

VIEW

Although some people might argue about how much art and music classes matter compared to other subjects, it's clear they do matter. Students who take these classes generally do better in school and are more likely to stay in school. In this way, art and music classes can be a path to future success for some students.

Studies show some ways art and music classes matter to students. However, there are some ways that can't be shown by numbers. Art and music classes help students see the world in new, creative ways. Why do you think art and music classes matter?

Know the Facts!

According to a 2015 study, 90 percent of Americans believe arts education is important.

Why are music and art classes cut?

- They cost too much money.

- Money needs to go to hiring more teachers for other subjects.

- They take time away from preparing for standardized tests.

Why **do** music and art classes matter?

- They make some students excited to go to school, which keeps them from **dropping out** of school.

- They teach students to value creativity, which is important for future jobs.

- They help students **do better** in other subjects.

These are just some of the points of view people have about art and music classes.

GLOSSARY

affect: To produce an effect on something.

at-risk: In danger of having trouble succeeding in school and in adulthood.

college: A school people can go to after high school.

debate: An argument or discussion about an issue, generally between two sides.

development: The act or process of growing or causing something to become more advanced.

focus: To direct attention or effort at something.

low-income: Earning little money through work.

low-performing: Relating to schools with students who don't get good grades on standardized tests or schools with a high dropout rate.

policy: A set of rules for how something is to be done.

program: The classes offered by a school in a certain subject.

For More
INFORMATION

WEBSITES

#MetKids
www.metmuseum.org/art/online-features/metkids/
The Metropolitan Museum of Art provides young visitors to their website with a fun way to learn more about art through an interactive map, videos, and other activities.

NGAkids Art Zone
www.nga.gov/education/kids.html
This part of the National Gallery of Art's website introduces kids to different art projects to go along with what they learn in art classes or to help them learn about art if they don't take art classes.

BOOKS

Durrie, Karen. *The Arts*. New York, NY: AV2 by Weigl, 2012.

Gardner, Jane P. *Music Science*. Broomall, PA: Mason Crest, 2016.

Walker, Kevin. *STEAM Guides in Inventions*. Mankato, MN: Rourke Educational Media, 2017.

INDEX